NATURE'S BOUNTY

A PRAIRIE FOOD CHAIN

A. D. Tarbox

A GREEN BOOK

SAUNDERS
BOOK COMPANY

Published by Saunders Book Company
27 Stewart Road
Collingwood ON Canada L9Y 4M7

Design by Rita Marshall
Production by CG Book
Printed in the United States of America

Photographs by Alamy (Blickwinkel; Don Johnston; Thomas
Shjarback); Corbis (Alan & Sandy Carey/Zeta; John
Carnemolla; W. Perry Conway; Joe McDonald; David
Muench; Richard Hamilton Smith); Getty Images (James
Balog; Peter Dennen; Jerry Dodrill; Terry Donnelly; Tim
Fitzharris; Brian G. Green; James Hager; S. Purdy
Matthews; Frank Oberle; Norbert Rosing/National
Geographic; Joel Sartore; Mark O. Thiessen; Tom Walker;
Ralph H. Wetmore II; Konrad Wothe)

*Special thanks to Dr. Brad Moon, Charlie Lee, Dr. Eva
Horne, Dr. Tim Maret, and Dr. David Long for their
assistance*

Copyright © 2009 Creative Education
Creative Education is an imprint of The Creative Company.
P.O. Box 227, Mankato, MN 56002

Library of Congress Cataloging-in-Publication Data
Tarbox, A. D. (Angelique D.)
A prairie food chain / by A. D. Tarbox.
p. cm. — (Nature's bounty)
Includes index.
ISBN 978-1-897563-12-0
1. Prairie ecology—Juvenile literature. 2. Food chains
(Ecology)—Juvenile literature. I. Title. II. Series.

QH541.5P7T37 2008
577.4'4—dc22   2007005682

First edition
9 8 7 6 5 4 3 2 1

Cover: A white-tailed deer fawn
Page 4: A bison skull
Pages 6–7: A hilly grassland

A bird swoops through the sky. In the depths of the sea, a whale dives. A wolf runs for miles across a snow-covered plain. They fly, swim, and travel in search of food. Animals spend most of their time looking for a plant or animal to eat, which will nourish them, provide energy, or help their off-spring survive. A food chain shows what living things in an area eat. Plants, called producers, are the first link on a food chain. Consumers, or animals that eat plants or other animals, make up the other links. The higher an animal is on the food chain, the less energy it receives from eating the animal below it. This is why there are more plants than plant eaters, and even fewer top consumers. Most animals eat more than one kind of plant or animal. Food webs show all of the possible food chains within a wildlife community.

Although the red-tailed hawk looks awkward when walking on the ground, it is a magnificent flier that spends most of its time soaring on currents of air.

When the first European settlers saw the North American prairie, they described it as a sea of grass. But the prairie has changed greatly since Europeans encountered it in the 1800s. The sea of grass, which used to dominate the middle of the North American continent, is now covered by roads and buildings, and many of the grasses have been replaced by corn or wheat. The prairie is now better known for what is no longer there, such as wolves and great herds of bison. Some scientists feel that the North American prairie is the most threatened **biome** on the planet. Despite the changes the prairie has undergone in the last 150 years, hundreds of **species** of plants, more than 80 species of **mammals**, and more than 300 kinds of birds still live there. These plants

Despite their name, grasslands are more than just grass. Many flowering plants—such as the purple lupines pictured here—add color and texture to the landscape.

The grasslands of Colorado feature the short grasses characteristic of the western North American prairie. Grasses grow taller as the prairie stretches eastward.

and animals make up numerous food chains, including one that begins with a tall grass and ends with a badger.

Bluestem Grass: Tall Prairie Plant

The North American prairie is a **temperate grassland** that today covers about 130,000 square miles (336,700 sq km). Before the 1800s, the prairie spanned approximately 600,000 square miles (1.6 million sq km). The prairie begins at the edge of the Rocky Mountains and extends eastward to Indiana, northward into Canada, and southward to Texas. Other parts of the world, such as Asia, South America, and Africa, have temperate grasslands as well. The prairies are called "steppes" in Asia, "pampas" in South America, and "veld" in southern Africa. The savanna in Africa is also a grassland, but it is usually in a **tropical** climate with more trees than a veld or a prairie. What all prairies have in common is that **perennial** grasses grow across the landscape, and under the grasses is fertile, black soil. This rich soil is why prairie land has historically been plowed up for use in agriculture.

The North American prairie is separated into three regions and today is about 23 percent shortgrass prairie, 70 percent mixed-grass, and 7 percent tallgrass. Before Europeans settled on the prairie, shortgrass spanned about 17 percent of the prairie, mixed-grass 40 percent, and tallgrass 43 percent. Scientists believe that short grasses first appeared in North America 30 million years ago and that the tallgrass prairie,

The pronghorn is considered the second-fastest land animal in the world (after the cheetah) and typically roams the prairie alone or in small groups during the summer.

where the predominant plant life consists of tall grasses such as Indian grass, is the youngest area on a prairie. It is also believed that ungulates, or hoofed animals such as bison, pronghorn, and elk, are part of the reason grasses were able to spread, as grass seeds were dispersed in the animals' feces or stuck to their fur.

Because the Rocky Mountains block rain clouds, only a small amount of moisture reaches the western edge of the prairie. This precipitation total is not enough to sustain forests but is the right amount for short grasses. The eastern side of the North American prairie receives more rainfall, which supports tall grasses such as bluestem. Strong winds and dry condi-

The middle of the North American prairie features especially fertile—and vulnerable— soil. The rich earth in this region supports lush, tall grasses and coneflowers.

tions are common on the prairie and create perfect conditions for fires to start and spread after lightning strikes. There are few trees on the prairie, and frequent fires prevent new ones from growing, but the burned plant material provides nourishment for grass seeds and roots.

There are thousands of years' worth of charcoal deposits under the North American prairie, which suggests that frequent fires may have helped shape and maintain the land. Since the mid-1800s, the prairie has been further shaped by cattle ranching and farming. Early clearing of prairie land was often mismanaged. In many places, the fertile topsoil was left exposed and lost **nutrients** to the wind. This mismanagement

of the land contributed to the **Dust Bowl** of the 1930s.

In the early 1800s, famed explorers Meriwether Lewis and William Clark were scouting for a northwest route to the Pacific Ocean for the United States government. During their journey, they wrote about the plants and animals they saw along the way. The tall prairie grass with the blue stem that reached high above their heads impressed them. Later, that blue color would give the bluestem grass its name. Lewis and Clark also noted how the bluestem crowded out other grasses. Little did they know that just over 30 years later, in 1837, the invention of the steel blade plow would make it possible for the tall grass to be easily tilled under, and that the prairie would be changed forever.

Earth Shaker

Bison, also called buffalo, are huge beasts that can weigh more than 1,000 pounds (450 kg) and reach heights of 6.5 feet (2 m). The early Plains Indians, such as the Arapaho and Lakota, depended on the grass-eating bison for meat, made pudding from the animal's blood, combed their hair with its dried tongue, and made clothes from its skin. Where the bison **migrated**, the Plains Indians followed. Bison usually move slowly, about two miles (3 km) a day, in large herds. However, if frightened, they may stampede in a thunderous, earth-shaking flight across the prairie. Bison follow a herd leader and can run up to 35 miles (56 km) per hour and maintain the pace for 30 minutes. The Plains Indians understood that bison followed their leader wherever he took them and sometimes used this knowledge to drive herds off cliffs. When European settlers first saw America's plains, more than 60 million bison roamed the land. By the late 1800s, only 500 bison were left, the vast herds having been hunted and casually slaughtered almost to extinction before the bison were finally given legal protection.

Bison, which eat mainly grass but also feed on twigs and leaves, today have a North American population of about 200,000 after being slaughtered nearly to extinction in the 1800s.

Many people consider the tallgrass prairie to be the truest form of prairie. Big bluestem grass is the predominant grass on the tallgrass prairie and can reach heights of 10 feet (3 m). It is sometimes called "turkey foot grass" because at the tip of the plant are spikelets, flowers that look like birds' feet. The spikelets produce the bluestem's seeds and bloom from August to November. Often described as feeling and looking hairy, the spikelets are green in the summer but turn a purplish color toward the fall. As a perennial grass, bluestem goes **dormant** in the winter and comes back every spring, each plant typically living about three years in all.

Like most prairie grasses, bluestem has evolved to handle dry conditions. The bluestem's height and narrow leaves are **adaptations** it has made to store and hoard water. It grows its roots deep into the ground where they can reach water. The roots also contain energy so that the grass can regrow after a fire. Before they became endangered (at risk of extinction), massive herds of bison used to feed on bluestem as they migrated across the prairie. Today, bluestem grass is consumed by a much smaller creature, an alien-looking animal with six legs and five eyes.

Differential Grasshopper: Frequent Flyer

During summer nights on the prairie, when the temperature is warm, people are likely to hear a unique kind of music. It isn't a band or an orchestra playing, but hundreds of male grasshoppers **stridulating** legs against wings, creating chirps and

With its great height, vast abundance, and high nutritional content, bluestem grass is a valuable food for many animals and is sometimes even baled as hay by farmers.

tweets in hopes of attracting a mate or claiming a territory.

Female differential grasshoppers are larger than males and reach lengths of up to two inches (5 cm). The differential grasshopper's size and coloring distinguish it from other grasshoppers. Its body comes in colors of pale green, yellow, or black, and its rear legs are marked by a herringbone pattern, which looks like rows of black lines that slope in opposite directions.

Like all insects, the differential grasshopper has three body parts: head, thorax, and abdomen. The grasshopper's head contains a brain and strong mandibles, or mouth parts, that it uses to bite and chew grass with a side-to-side motion. Extending out from its head are sensitive smell organs called antennae, which tell the grasshopper if a plant it has touched is worth eating or not. Differential grasshoppers have five eyes. Two of them are large, **compound eyes** the grasshopper uses to see objects. The other three are so small that they are barely noticeable and are used not for vision but for detecting light. One is located between the grasshopper's compound eyes, and the other two are on the sides of its head. The differential grasshopper also has an exoskeleton, or hard outer shell, and six legs. Its two rear legs, attached to the thorax, are very large and are used for jumping. A differential grasshopper can jump 20 times higher and farther than the length of its body, and its two pairs of wings help it fly. The abdomen holds the grasshopper's tympanal organ, which serves as its ears. The grasshopper breathes through tiny holes called spiracles that dot its sides.

There are thousands of grasshopper species found all around the world. The differential grasshopper (pictured) is one of the most common North American species.

Male and female grasshoppers pair off and mate for up to 24 hours. After breeding, the female finds a suitable place to deposit her eggs, usually near grass. She leans her body against a stalk of grass and, using a tubelike organ called an ovipositor, deposits up to 190 eggs in the dirt, surrounding them with a foamy substance called a pod. The pod hardens and protects the eggs. Adult grasshoppers do not often live through the winter on the plains; it is simply too cold. But the eggs laid in the fall usually survive the winter and hatch in the spring. Newly hatched grasshoppers are called nymphs, and they are often attacked and eaten by ants. Able to jump from birth, the young grasshoppers feed on grasses and **forbs**. They molt, or shed their skin, every week as they quickly grow. After five molts, or about 40 days after hatching, they develop wings and become adults able to stridulate and fly.

Besides stridulating, differential grasshoppers communicate with each other by crepitating, a noisy behavior in which they open their wings and then snap them shut. They also communicate visually with one another by flashing their wings and legs. These methods of communication are used to attract other grasshoppers, to threaten a potential rival in mating season, or to defend food. There are more than 10,000 species of grasshoppers in the world, and each, including the differential grasshopper, is thought to have its own language.

Adult differential grasshoppers fly to cool down when the summer heat rises above 86 °F (30 °C) or to escape from **predators** such as prairie dogs and prairie chickens. Pilots flying as high as 1,400 feet (427 m) have seen differential grasshoppers flying along beside their airplanes. Differential grasshoppers also fly, sometimes in large groups, when they want to migrate. They may travel as far as 130 miles (209 km) in their search for better feeding areas.

Ravenous grasshoppers can quickly devastate wild plants and farmers' crops when they gather in large swarms, consuming hundreds of thousands of tons in food.

Differential grasshoppers begin their day at dawn. During the night, the grasshoppers' body temperature drops as they rest near a stalk of bluestem grass or at the top of it. The grasshoppers move to a sunny spot in the morning, either on the ground or somewhere on the big bluestem, to help them warm up. After an hour or two of basking, the grasshoppers climb to the top of the bluestem grass, tapping their antennae against the plant as they ascend. The grasshoppers like what their antennae smell and take a bite of the bluestem. They make a mess as their jaws rip and chew pieces of the bluestem, and uneaten fragments of the grass accumulate on the ground, creating leaf litter. Also consuming farm plants, a swarm of differential grasshoppers can destroy a field of wheat or corn in a few days. As they eat, though, differential grasshoppers have to beware of a ravenous predator under the prairie grass that knows how to stop them from jumping away.

Prairie Decomposer

Prairie earthworms are about the length of a ball-point pen. However, earthworms in other parts of the world, such as the giant earthworms of Australia, can be longer than a couch. Earthworms have no eyes, ears, or skeleton, but their strong muscles enable them to wriggle through dirt. They can live for as long as 10 years, but they have many enemies. Hedgehogs, shrews, and moles eat them underground, and when earthworms surface after a rainstorm to avoid drowning, birds such as robins grab them by their tail. A tug-of-war match ensues as the earthworm tries to get back into the soil, but the bird usually emerges the winner. Living in the soil provides earthworms with dead plants and soil to eat, which they suck up with tiny lips and drag into their burrows. Earthworms play a very important role on the prairie by breaking down dead grass. A single earthworm's nibbling, burrowing, and fecal matter improves more than half a pound (0.3 kg) of soil a year.

Earthworms benefit the prairie food web in different ways, both enriching the soil to help plant growth and serving as a food source for animals such as hungry robins.

Prairie Shrew: Tiny Biter

Many scientists believe that the first mammals to flourish after the days of the dinosaurs were shrew-like animals. In North America, fossil remains of shrews have been found that date back to the Eocene era of 55 million years ago. Perhaps the shrews' small size, underground lifestyle, and preferred prey—primarily insects—made it possible for them to survive what the huge **reptiles** could not.

The prairie shrew is distinguished from other shrews by its long tail. The total length of this hand-sized shrew, including its tail, is approximately four inches (10 cm), and it weighs about as much as a nickel. Cinnamon-colored fur covers most of its body, while the hair on its belly is usually gray. The prairie shrew has 32 teeth, two more than other

Although the prairie shrew is believed to be a rather bad-tasting animal, it is still preyed upon by a range of grassland hunters that includes owls, foxes, and snakes.

species of shrews, and iron pigments make the tips of its teeth red-colored.

Prairie shrews have long, pointy noses and an excellent sense of smell, but their small eyes do not see well. Some kinds of shrews live underground or climb trees, but prairie shrews use their short legs and strong claws to make paths, called runways, in grass debris. Their nests of grass look like birds' nests, which they build under the cover of logs, stones, or tall grasses such as bluestem. Prairie shrews prefer a solitary life and get together only to mate.

After mating in the summer with several males, the female

prairie shrew gives birth three weeks later to about eight offspring called pups. She has up to three pregnancies a year. Shrew pups often caravan, lining up with their snouts touching the rear end of the sibling in front of them and moving through the runways like schoolchildren walking the halls in straight, orderly lines. After three to four weeks of nursing, the caravanning and playing stops. As if a switch has been flipped inside them, the young shrews suddenly realize it is time to live alone, and they disperse. They will now fight their littermates if they come across them again.

Shrews are **territorial** about their runways, nests, and food, such as beetles, earthworms, and grasshoppers. They avoid other shrews or defend their territories by biting. Shrews spend a lot of time hidden under grass debris or in under-

ground burrows to avoid predators such as short-eared owls and swift foxes. Finding cover is their preferred method for avoiding predators, as they usually cannot outrun pursuers. When prairie shrews are in their summer breeding season, some predators avoid them. Glands on the shrews swell during this time, casting a pungent odor. Scientists believe the stinky smell helps attract other shrews while also discouraging predators, thereby helping the shrew live long enough to mate. Shrews can live up to 15 months, and their numbers are abundant on the prairie.

A prairie shrew's high **metabolism** requires it to hunt a lot. In fact, a shrew is considered to be in starvation mode if it

Swift Striker

Red-tailed hawks are often seen perched on telephone poles along the prairie. From these man-made structures, they can scan for their favorite prey: prairie dogs, rats, snakes, and birds such as prairie grouse and pheasants. When fully grown at two years old, the hawks grow their signature red tail feathers. Their white chest and 48-inch (122 cm) wingspan make recognizing these large birds rather easy. The red-tailed hawk is one of the few birds capable of hovering like a helicopter. The hawks' eyesight is eight times better than that of humans, and their ability to capture prey with precise, missile-like aerial strikes makes them popular birds in North American falconry (the sport of hunting prey with birds, which was very popular in the days of medieval kings). Apprentice falconers—persons training to be masters in the sport—commonly use red-tailed hawks. Falconers often release red-tailed hawks back into the wild because they never become truly tamed, and the birds quickly return to their natural ways.

The raspy, screaming call of the red-tailed hawk is regarded as the classic bird of prey cry and is commonly used in movies to represent hawks and eagles of all kinds.

has not eaten in 10 hours. The shrew does not hibernate in the winter but searches for insect eggs and **larvae**. A shrew that lives on the northern parts of the plains, where the winters can be more severe, sometimes goes into **Dehnel's effect**. During this time, it loses as much as 40 percent of its weight, and its skull and organs actually shrink as an adaptation to survive while taking in less food. When spring returns, bringing with it more food, such as the differential grasshopper, the shrew fattens up.

Shrews are constantly searching for food. They are aggressive predators who like to hunt at night but will also search for food during the day. Shrews are mostly insect carnivores, but they also eat mice, plant seeds, and carrion (the rotting flesh of dead animals). Hunting alone, running like thieves from grass runways to leaf cover, they look nervous as they search for food. Using their excellent sense of smell and their **vibrissa**, prairie shrews can quickly detect and locate prey such as the differential grasshopper. Prairie shrews will attempt to eat any insect they come across that is small and moving.

When a prairie shrew sees a differential grasshopper, it runs at the insect and tries to catch it with its mouth. The grasshopper's only defense against a shrew is to fly or jump away. Moving swiftly, the prairie shrew bites the grasshopper's legs so that it cannot hop away. Once the grasshopper cannot jump, the shrew bites off the grasshopper's head and eats the insect's insides. A prairie shrew may eat four to six grasshoppers a day. As it returns to its nest after eating,

Although a bull snake can be intimidating when it assumes a defensive posture, its lack of venom makes it much less dangerous than the similar-looking rattlesnake.

though, the prairie shrew must watch out for a slithering guest that may be waiting in ambush.

Bull Snake: Hissing Constrictor

Bull snakes are non-venomous reptiles that are frequently mistaken for rattlesnakes because, like rattlesnakes, bull snakes shake their tail when threatened. Like many snakes, bull snakes can easily move through thick grass or climb rocks and trees. How do animals without legs, arms, or wings do this? The physical design of the bull snakes' body enables them to do what may initially seem impossible. Bull snakes are able to move forward by pushing approximately 9,000 muscles and scales against a surface. With about 225 **vertebrae**, bull snakes have the flexibility to bend like string around branches, curl tight, and straighten without injury.

Bull snakes, sometimes called pine or gopher snakes, have multicolored scales of red, brown, white, and yellow, all with a keeled, or unshiny, appearance that helps them blend in with the grasses of the plains. As constrictors, bull snakes kill their prey, such as rabbits, pocket gophers, or prairie dogs, by biting them and then suffocating them inside tight coils.

Bull snakes, like all snakes, do not have eyelids and therefore cannot blink. Instead, they have a plastic-like scale over each eye that offers protection like an eyelid. Bull snakes use their sense of smell to help them find prey, but they do not have a nose. Rather, a forked tongue that the snakes constantly flick out of their mouth smells by taking chemical samples from the air. Located in the roof of the reptiles'

Alert Rodent

Prairie dogs eat grass, and many make their homes on the shortgrass to mixed-grass regions of the prairie. They have famously complex social and vocal behaviors. Prairie dogs are plentiful and live underground in extended family groups called colonies that cooperate with each other by keeping a lookout for predators such as coyotes. A prairie dog uses barks and chuckling sounds if it wants to convey an alarm call announcing that an enemy, such as a hawk, badger, or ferret, is near. At one time, the most common predators of prairie dogs were the black-footed ferret and the gray wolf. The gray wolf was killed off from the prairie more than 100 years ago, and the black-footed ferret is almost extinct. About 20 years ago, scientists rounded up the last remaining black-footed ferrets and began breeding them in zoos to try to save them. Since 1991, small numbers of black-footed ferrets have been returned to the prairie, where they live inside prairie dog tunnels and prey on prairie dogs at every opportunity.

Prairie dog colonies can be huge. The largest prairie dog colony ever recorded covered 25,000 square miles (65,000 sq km) and included about 400 million animals!

stretch its jaws as wide as necessary to make its prey fit. The snake won't have to eat again for a while. It will go back to its den or find another secluded place in which to rest. Even at rest, though, the bull snake can't let its guard down, as there is a much more powerful prairie animal that knows how to dig out an underground snake.

Badger: Prairie Digger

Along with the coyote, the American badger is one of the top predators of the prairie. It is about as heavy as a medium-sized dog and measures about 34 inches (86 cm) from head to tail. With its black and white stripes, a badger's face looks like that of a skunk. However, the rest of its bulky body is a shaggy gray, brown, or reddish color.

With their short, powerful legs, partially webbed five digits, and super-long claws, badgers are expert diggers, and they spend a lot of their time moving soil and making tunnels. Their small eyes are protected from the dirt by a nictitating membrane, which is like an extra eyelid. Badgers can see objects up close but not at great distances. They have good hearing, but their ability to smell is by far their best sense.

Badgers are relatively clean animals, especially for as much time as they spend digging and living in dirt. They groom themselves by licking their fur, swallowing the loose hair. They also bury their feces much like house cats do. They do not hibernate in the winter but instead rest in a **torpid** state.

Like many animals that spend a lot of time burrowing, the badger has a broad, flattened head. This helps it push and squeeze into the ground, like the blade of a shovel.

During this time, hunkered down in a den, a badger's body temperature drops to about 48 °F (9 °C), and its heart beats at half its normal rate. To conserve energy, badgers sleep in this torpid state for about 29 hours at a time before hunting again.

Near a badger's rear end are glands that produce a foul odor called musk. Badgers squirt musk on grass to attract mates and to mark their territory. After mating in the summer or fall, male and female badgers go their separate ways. American badgers live as solitary animals except when the female rears her young. Fertilized eggs do not start developing in the female until February of the following year. Finally, five weeks after that, two or three silver-furred baby badgers, called kits, are born.

As the kits get older, their mother brings them dead animals, such as ground squirrels, that she has killed for them to eat. When the kits are two months old, they leave their mother and strike out on their own. Only about 25 percent of badgers live past their first year. Many die of disease, and young badgers can fall prey to animals such as great horned owls.

Using their massive claws, badgers dig underground burrows, often beside slopes. Sometimes they take over the home of another animal, such as the burrow of a ground squirrel, and make it larger. They push and kick dirt from their den and even move rocks. Badgers also make underground tunnels, often connecting multiple dens inside their territory. They line their burrows with grass and often use a different den every day.

Whenever badgers are digging, curious coyotes may be watching nearby. There is an interesting connection between the coyote and the badger. At one time, the coyote was rarely seen on the prairie. However, after wolves were killed off on the prairie by human hunters, the coyote population boomed and spread. The coyote and badger occasionally eat each other, but they also like to eat the same prey, such as ground squirrels. Sometimes, as a badger digs up an underground nest, a coyote stands by and watches. When the rodents try to escape, the coyote snatches whatever runs past the badger.

Since badgers are at the top of the prairie food chain, their biggest threat is humans, who sometimes kill them for their fur. Badgers are not fast runners, so they sometimes rely on their speed at digging to escape threats. They may raise their fur to look larger and more intimidating, and if harassed by an enemy, badgers will attack and fight fiercely. Under all that fur, they have very loose skin, and if they are grabbed, they can twist their bodies around and deliver a nasty bite.

An omnivore, the badger may eat fruits and roots in addition to its diet of meat. As it digs in underground burrows looking

The weeks that badger siblings spend together are the most social times of their lives, as the kits soon go their separate ways and live in isolation the rest of their days.

35

for prey, a badger may come across a resting bull snake in the summer or a hibernating snake in the winter. The bull snake tries to scare off the badger with its loud hissing and shakes its tail so it sounds like a poisonous rattlesnake. But the badger is not intimidated because it kills and eats rattlesnakes, too. The badger nails the bull snake to the ground with its claws and spears through the snake's body with its teeth. The parts of the snake the badger does not eat may be taken to its den to be eaten later.

The bull snake in the badger's belly is linked to the prairie shrew, the differential grasshopper, and the bluestem grass in the prairie food chain. One day, when the badger dies, perhaps due to injury or disease, its body will decompose and

Few animals can match the badger in digging speed. A badger can dig a burrow faster than a man with a shovel could, perhaps finding a snake to eat in the process.

provide nutrients for new bluestem grass to grow. And the prairie food chain will continue.

Big bluestem grass has deep roots, which enable it to survive foraging animals and summer wildfires and then grow back to help start prairie food chains anew.

Africa's Grasslands

The temperate grassland of South Africa is known as the veld. Much of it is often located near mountain slopes.

Similar to the North American prairie, the veld has short and tall grasses and has been shaped by fires. Some sec-

tions of the veld are covered by only one species of grass because of mismanaged fires set by humans. Africa is

probably best known for its tropical grassland, the savanna, which has more trees than the veld or prairies. Herds of

hoofed animals such as zebras and wildebeests, and herbivores such as African elephants and rhinoceroses, graze

on the savanna's grasses. Often nearby is a lion pride that includes hungry and watchful lionesses. As the lionesses

move closer to the zebra, gazelle, or wildebeest herd, they stalk slowly and spread like a fan, advancing in a line. An

old, injured, or newborn animal from the herd is chosen, and when the lionesses have crept as close to it as they

can, they rush forward in a swift burst. One lioness clamps on to the animal's throat, and the others leap on the

prey. Within minutes, the animal is dragged down.

The African savanna is quite different from the North American prairie. The savanna is warm year-round, is sparsely settled, and is home to such predators as lions.

Although wildfires can be deadly, threatening both wildlife and human property, fire can also benefit the prairie, destroying dry grasses and promoting fresh plant growth.

Glossary

adaptations – changes an animal species makes over time—such as growing thicker fur or eating other foods—to survive in its environment

biome – a region of the world that is differentiated from others by its predominant plant life and climate

compound eyes – eyes that feature numerous smaller compartments; they help animals such as insects detect motion

Dehnel's effect – a survival mode in small mammals that helps them live through severe food shortages by decreasing their body weight and bones by as much as 50 percent

dormant – a state of reduced body activity in which an organism does not grow and its metabolism slows down

Dust Bowl – region of the central U.S. where drought and soil erosion caused dust storms in the 1930s

forbs – broad-leafed plants, such as the purple prairie clover, that are not considered grasses and that many might consider weeds; forbs are important food plants for many animals

larvae – the early stage of growth for some animals such as insects; the young animal often does not look like it will as an adult

mammals – backboned animals that have hair and nurse their young with milk

metabolism – the chemical and physical process inside an organism that regulates the amount of energy used for activities and sustaining life

migrated – moved from one climate or location to another to find food or to breed

nutrients – minerals, vitamins, and other substances that provide an organism with what it needs to live, grow, and flourish

perennial – a plant that stays alive through all the seasons and lives for several years

predators – animals that live by killing for their food

reptiles – cold-blooded animals that have a backbone and scaled skin or a hard shell; examples include snakes and turtles

species – animals that have similar characteristics and are able to mate with each other

stridulating – making noise by rubbing together certain body parts

temperate grassland – a region of the world with warm summer temperatures and about 20 inches (51 cm) of rain or snow a year; temperate grasslands support grasses and have few trees but very fertile soil

territorial – animals that have an attachment to a property and mark the boundaries of it, usually with feces and urine, and often will fight to keep it

torpid – a state of rest in which an animal does not eat for days at a time, and its body temperature and heart rate drop to conserve energy; it usually occurs during winter months when food is scarce

tropical – characterized by year-round temperatures above 64 °F (18 °C) and frequent rainfall

vertebrae – The bony segments that form the backbone

vibrissa – stiff hairs that grow on many animals such as shrews and cats; they are usually located on the face and are sensitive to touch

A prairie dog feeding

Selected Bibliography

Berman, Ruth. *American Bison.* Minneapolis: Carolrhoda Books, 1992.

Klobuchar, Lisa. *Badgers and Other Mustelids.* Chicago: World Book, 2006.

Llewellyn, Claire. *Earthworms.* Danbury, Conn.: Franklin Watts, 2002.

Pascoe, Elaine. *Crickets and Grasshoppers.* Woodbridge, Conn.: Blackbirch Press, 1999.

Patent, Dorothy Hinshaw. *Prairies.* New York: Holiday House, 1996.

Wilson, Don E., and Sue Ruff. *The Smithsonian Book of North American Mammals.* Washington, D.C.: Smithsonian Institution Press, 1999.

Woodward, Susan L. *Biomes of Earth.* Westport, Conn.: Greenwood Press, 2003.

A scaled quail

badgers 31, 33–34, 36
  burrows 33, 36
  digging 33, 34, 36
  kits 33
  musk 33
  plant diet 36
  prey 33, 36
  reproduction 33
  size 33
  territories 33
bison 11, 12, 14, 17
black-footed ferrets 31
bluestem grass 12, 13, 17, 19, 22, 36
  color 13, 17
  height 17
  life span 17

roots 17
spikelets 17
bull snakes 27–29, 33, 36
  color 27
  constriction 27, 29
  eggs 28–29
  enemies 28
  life span 29
  prey 27, 29
  reproduction 28
  sense of smell 27–28
  size 29
coyotes 31, 33, 34
differential grasshoppers 17–19, 23, 27, 36
  color 17
  communication 17, 18
  eggs 18
  enemies 18, 19
  feeding 19
  flying 17, 18, 19
  jumping 17, 18
  migration 19
  reproduction 18
  size 17
earthworms 21, 23
fires 13, 17, 38

lions 38
North American prairie
  human impact on 13
  mixed-grass 12, 31
  precipitation 12
  shortgrass 12, 31
  size 11
  tallgrass 12, 17
pampas 11
prairie dogs 19, 25, 31
prairie shrews 22–23, 27, 29, 33, 36
  caravanning 23
  enemies 23
  hunting 23, 27
  life span 23
  nests 22
  prey 23, 27
  pups 23
  reproduction 22–23
  runways 22, 23, 27
  size 22
  territories 23
red-tailed hawks 25
Rocky Mountains 12
savanna 12, 38
soil 12, 13, 21
steppes 11
veld 12, 38
wolves 11, 31, 34

A dragonfly on prairie grass